CLOT AND MARROW

CLOT AND
MARROW

ES FOONG

RECENT
WORK
PRESS

Clot and Marrow
Recent Work Press
Canberra, Australia

Copyright © Es Foong, 2023

ISBN: 9780645651287 (paperback)

A catalogue record for this
book is available from the
National Library of Australia

Cover image by 'Frangellina', 2017
Cover design: Recent Work Press
Set by Recent Work Press

recentworkpress.com

For Arthur,
who is in every page of my life, written, unwritten,
and those yet to be written.

These poems were written, performed and lived on
the lands of the Wurundjeri Woi-wurrung people
of the Kulin nation. I acknowledge the Traditional
Owners of these unceded lands and pay my respects
to Elders past and present.

Contents

in

hold

out

am breath

am morning tender-filtered slats.
am blackbird raucous-relish in nest.
am knee lament-locked and loosened.
am thigh caress-tender under sheets.
am body down-beat slump-still.
      am breath.
      in.
            hold.
      out.

am screen wade-text flow-shock.
am coffee bitter-vital throat-sup.
am task-list slow-drown smile.
am phone-mask ersatz-ego.
am neck lock-space dense-bound.
      am breath.
      in.
            hold.
      out.

am grass kindle-spark ignite.
am lead-weight chest rage-tight.
am arched-spine curdle-bound.
am sorrow-skip deflect-remember.
am dispirit past midnight.
     am breath.
     in.
        hold.
     out.

am sunbeam dusk-glow tingle.
am tears mellow-ripple knot-ease.
am finger-tips curled cherish-warmth.
am throat-lark hum-trill hush.
am dream-wing slow-joy radiate.
     am breath.
     in.
        hold.
     out.

in

Where We Keep the Barbies

This is where we live.

This is where we keep the Barbies,
still in their boxes, corners peeling.

We play Lego here, blocks stacked each day,
dismantled every night, every piece has its place.

Build houses with symmetrical roofs,
no time for trees or dinosaurs.

Build a neat home for the dolly mommy,
daddy and tiny baby with its bottle.

This is where we keep the skipping rope, rubber ball
and bat, outside toys we don't take outside.

This is where friends sit, the sofa wrapped in plastic,
wiped down when friendly intruders leave.

We sit at the edge of things,
hope they don't ask to use the bathroom.

Dream of houses with asymmetrical roofs,
where our Barbies sprawl on Lego couches akimbo.

Clot and Marrow

when you are five
                    and you love marmalade
                                        on toast for breakfast

and your father whom you've never
                                heard raise his voice
                                                                                    breaks
a chair
                            in the next room

and your little sister
                            the size of a watermelon
                                        and smeared in jam
                                                                            reaches out
for your wrist

and your mother scoops you both up
                                                    bundles you into the car

            drives down the street
                                    in a way that even your five year old
self understands
                                                        as a death wish

and you don't remember how you
                                    ended up safely
                                                            back in bed
you look up to see a rare

                                                        evening star

                when you are five and this happens
                your bones are still malleable enough
                that you can
                                find the anger in yourself
                                            lock it into your bones
                                    knit it into your marrow
                                            and once you're done

                                            you train your eyes on that distant
star
                determined to follow it

your most vivid colours bleed out of you
                                            each month along with
                                                                    clot and marrow

there is nothing left for your art
                                                            but pastel
                                and shades of grey

I, Monstrous, Insist on Being in Every Poem that I Write

I am not supposed to be in this moment
and yet here I am,
standing in front of the refrigerator
with a small plastic spork in one hand
and a little red bowl in another.

I am not supposed to be in this moment
and I'm not, not the slightest recollection
of this moment or the one before
when mum got home from work and asked
'Why do I smell throw up?'

No recollection either, of telling mum the story
of how Ying Che Che made me swallow
my own expelled nausea, scooped
from the sink into my little red bowl
and fed back to me with my spork.

But I remember the day she left
two years later, me standing at the window
crying, they had to hold me back
from thrusting my fat little belly
into the door, I remember how

she looked back at me before she drove away.

Collections of Wild Wants

We are energy conversion machines
Turning sunlight into kinetic force
Consuming nature and spitting out action
Each, a little god, a whirling dervish

We are receptacles of wonder
Staring out at the new-old world
Innocent and unable to conceive
An end to this cosmic dream

We are all collections of wild wants
Mad desires churning under thin skin
Sparks from the underworld
Feed our psyches' burning dreams

Back to You

No light, no sound, no air, no touch, no lingering scent of vanilla and lemons as you brush your fingers through my hair, long hair, brown hair, straight hair, caught up in a bun so I look more grown-up.

Short skirt, long shirt, tall shoes, unsteady gait, strawberry pink lips, glowing lips, puffed up lips, kissable lips you say, biting, pinching, licking in the car on the way to the movie and later, at the restaurant, you bring oysters to my lips, order me cocktails in tall frosted glasses rimmed with salt, listening all the while as I babble on about what I want to be when I graduate, leave school, leave—you.

But I'll come back to you, I say, I will always come back to you.

Afterwards there is your room, naked lightbulb swinging against a smoke stained ceiling, my head light, my stomach lurching, my skin hungry, my mouth hungry, my whole body hungry and spinning, light and spinning, sweat slicked caresses, thin mattress, bones jolting, against metal.

A lightbulb cracks.
A body falls.
There is no light.
No sound.
No air.
No touch.

Cleaner Feelings

The bruise on your thigh
just at the hem
of your skirt.
I saw it as you were dancing.

I wanted to kiss it,
press my thumb
into blue blood.
Slap your wound red again.

I want to be different,
to be capable of quiet
without a muzzle.
To stop feeding

before the fear of lightness
demands its sugar tax.
To let crumbs linger
under the tongue.

I want to have dirtier
thoughts, cleaner feelings,
a range of reaction not so closely
bound to wounds.

Scream, burn it all down,
flail and let them think you mad
or better yet, stupid.

In the silence between beats
sing back at the dance
floor, in blue blood.

Kindergarten Taught Me Everything I Need to Know About Life

There is the giraffe slide
Here is the caterpillar swing set
No one plays on the monkey bars
But there's always a line
At the carousel shaped like a cat

There is our Teacher, Mrs Thong!
Here is where we wash our hands
My new lunch box
A sandwich of Gardenia bread
with Kraft cheese and Goober grape

There is Min Min who says
I'm too tomboy to play on the giraffe
Here is Kevin who shoos girlie me
from the swing set
I can always monkey on the monkey bars

There the girls in their dresses
Here the boys in their shorts
Mummy with her perm,
Daddy in his tie
And me on the monkey bars
Learning to contort

hold

When You Ask Me

When you ask me where I come from,
what do you mean—exactly?
Just now, as I walked through the door?
The suburb I live in?
Where I was born?
Where I keep my best dishes?
All
  the
    places
      I keep a toothbrush?

Do you mean rather, where my parents were born?
My ancestors?
The provenance of my descendency?
How many migrations back would you have me go?
The last plane?
The ship before that?
The long march through starved valleys?
The time of the cave clan tending
a single lightning-lit fire?

When you ask me where I come from,
what will you take from this answer?
What sacrifice would sate your curiosity?
What will it take to sooth your discomfort
with my dissonance from your expectations?
How much of my skin will you
blanket in your assumptions,
in half understood historical facts,
in dimly conscious but firmly held stereotypes?

Do we all have a collection
of gilded cages in our minds?
Cages we are eager to fill with specimens?
For all that we pride ourselves
on the sophistication and gradation of our opinions,
they are all still cages.

Can we crack open those doors?
Can we allow the stale air
to rush out of our lungs,
to animate the songs we sing
when we ask each other
where do you come from?

When you ask me where I come from,
perhaps what you mean to say is this:
where does your heart now reside?
What journeys has it been on?
What sights has it seen to shape its contours?
What curios do you fit into the cracks and ledges
left over from heart break?

Perhaps you mean to ask:
What rhythms do you hear in the womb?
In your own, your mother's,
her mother's and her mother's before,
what rhythms have become
the music of your blood?

How does this music syncopate
with the beating of your own heart?
Is it wild or tame?

When your heart sings,
does it do so in a key foreign
to where your feet stand?
Or does it sing in perfect harmony?
Does your chest strain from the stress
of holding in symphonies different
to the common ear?
Or does your heart sing
to hear itself at home?

Perhaps, when you ask me where I come from,
you mean to say:
do you have the keys
to the locked chambers of my heart?
Do I have the keys to yours?
Shall we compare
the rusty loops of our keychains?

Perhaps, when you ask me where I come from,
you mean to say:
What poetry does your soul dream in?
Shall we share the way home?

Women's Histories

Lock door.
Pull curtains
tight.
Tighter.
Tuck knife
under pillow.
Pull children
close.
Closer.
Wait,
for morning.

That Park

for Eurydice Dixon

I stand shoulder to shoulder
with a thousand strangers
in the simulated dark.
Why are we standing here?
I mean I remember the vigil,
but what an odd venue,
this open, busy park.

Together we grow a silence.
Perhaps now, I can finally
try to think, to remember.
But I can't help straining
to hear, it's always there
if you listen, it's
always happening.

Always the other cries
from clubs and pubs
and streets and alleys
and cars and corridors
and living rooms
and bedrooms.
Why are we standing here?

As I cycle home,
I measure the darkness
against the hour
(just dinner time?

Is that early *enough*?)
Wonder if I should have
taken a another path,
braved traffic instead.

Too many bushes here,
too many shadows,
every headlight
a passing threat.
The cold plucks at my cuticles,
fingers and toes,
I will never be warm again.
Why am I here?

Later that night,
tucked *safe* in bed
I feel warm
for the first time
that day.
I finally remember why:
                    That. Park.
Open and friendly:
                    That's. Where. She. Was.

It's always too warm
under here, too cozy
in the dark, that's why
I sleep with one foot
over the covers.
Untucked, I remember
always to be awake,
because I'm not
supposed to be here.

Wherever this is,
we're not supposed to be here.

Gasping

I've got this panic
        stricken feeling,
        I've failed.
If only I said
the right things,
screamed at the proper
pitch, I would not be
        drowning,
        with the rest

of the world and here
I am as the
        waters rise,
        vainly flailing
for passing driftwood,
reaching out for what

splinters and floating
trash might prove
        I don't deserve
        this end,

I just want to breathe, and
it's never been about
who is worthy,
        we are the same
species, the same
sentience, the same
flailing,
        drowning soul.

My Words Through Your Ears

You said in the meeting that the female client was hot.
I don't know to be more offended you've made the first

consideration of a woman's worth her fuck-ability,
or that by saying it in front of me, you deem that I am not.

'It's just a joke,' you say with a sideways glance in my direction.
'I'm having some fun with the boys. I'm a good bloke.'

Don't mind the bitch-face boss, not gonna bust your ass.
I just don't think it's funny. And no, I'm not angry. I'm tired.

I've crafted an entire person for your consumption. Gave
myself a footy allegiance, cuss words, brass balls, the lot.

To be fair, my act was never that good. No kids, no guns, no SUV.
No lil' lady waiting at home. My curves like the lithesome strippers

up there, but with too many awkward political angles.
And I may have given myself away with one too many eye rolls,

when you were just being a good bloke and I refused
to get the joke. But honestly, I'm not angry, I'm just tired.

We were friendly so I thought we were friends. You thought so too,
because you told me the truth when I asked, 'Why do they hear you,

friend, when they don't hear me? Is it because I'm …'
You said, 'That might have something to do with it.'

But I've worked so hard to make my differences invisible,
I'm a man for all the important intents! You said,

'That might have something to do with it—too.' I should
thank you for your honesty, but can't look you in the eye.

You were a good bloke, faithful witness to my humiliation.
You think I'm angry at you. I'm not. I'm just tired.

When I hear my words through your ears,
when I hear the alienation, but not the tears,

I can understand why you would think the likes of me would be
snatching the rice—sorry, bread, from the mouth of your babes.

There's no use explaining that I'm just like you, just want to live
in the house, with the car, the big screen tv, and maybe do a lil'
good.

These links are tenuous, will not bridge the differences that run
deeper than skin. When you're with me you don't know

how to be a good bloke. Believe me when I say I get the joke.
And I'm not angry. I'm just tired.

Elephant

i.
The words catch in your lengthy trunk.
The words catch in the bulbous
end of things.
The words catch in ears immense,
'We die, we will die, we are dying.'

ii.
You are the snake in fertile fields.
You are pressed lips in company,
breath stopped mid-kiss,
your silent mouth spits,
time is all, time means nothing.

iii.
The cobwebs we wrap around our eyes,
a mask, a shield, a sticky trap,
an ancient slow poison, its
tendrils curve around our sight.
We choose blindness before the end.

iv.
The pumping of our hearts, we know
we do not determine the cadence.
The beat is its own drum.
There is a bullet hidden
in this noisy toy.

v.
The words catch in the stroke of throat.
The words catch at the tip of ancient tusk.
The words catch in eyes tear dewed.
They catch the scattered years,
barren years, wombed in silence.

Devastation

The tide pulls out sometimes
So I can be the delicate woman
You desire of me
Sometimes the moon
Pulls the tide in
So my ears fill with salt water
So the fluids unbalance me
And the roar of the waves
Roaring in and roaring out
Has no way of escaping
But through my mouth
Into your ears
I mean to devastate you

Pregnancy and the Bikini Wax

One thing I don't write about
is pregnancy
the other is the bikini wax
this may be because I've never
experienced either
it may also be because I think
about both a lot
occasionally at the same time

the thing about pregnancy
and the bikini wax
is that you have to wonder, don't you?
when you're female identified
and of a certain age
what it would have been like
if it would have made you happier
better, and more loved

you were so certain once
it just was not for you
but you have to wonder, don't you?
now its too late
or is it? always that past midnight
gut churn, palm itch, eye burn
query: now it's too late
is it?

you've watched friends take
the treacherous leap, to emerge
exhausted, teary eyed
always the immutable law
of change and growth applies
and you, you'll grow old
alone, in some nursing home
hairy.

one thing I don't write about
is pregnancy
the other is the bikini wax
and I don't think I'll ever do it again
but I'll always think
about both a lot
because I've never tried either
and that marks me

Venus

I would rise out of the waves,
    clean and gleaming,
        clamshell perfect.
   Your idea of poise
    reflected pearlescent
        on alabaster skin.
Ringlets of gold or bronze,
   foil for your desires,
  but never a stray or split mane.

    Perfect love, devoted and
   wholly single hearted.
    Perfect rage, undeniable as fire,
  immoveable as your gaze.
I'd live only between
    these velvet curtains.

Have you see naught of the
   mess,
     ambivalence,
   this business of weakness,
    of fruit rotten from neglect,
   of lilies thrown at my feet
    now bleeding yellow
  on a linen tablecloth,
the stuttering of doubt on repeat,
  the steady shuffling of sloth.

I would rise from the foam
                    coyly frothed,
and have you consider only
   the careful placement of my hands.

Don't ask for me to turn around.
I have run out of discretion.
If you are one to declare
      that you can forge a web
      strong enough to bear my secrets
                  then friend,
         you are wrong.

Closed for Renovations

My favourite place to go alone
was always 3 am. My witching
hour, they say that's when the calls
to the suicide hotlines spike, that's
when my feet most often slapped
tarmac, looking for lost sleep,
looking for signs of life, looking for
the detritus of human achievement
without human presence. I once
walked all the way down Broadway
in Manhattan, darkness made friendly
by loneliness, tourist footsteps washed
into gutters by street lamps. There at
Times Square, a homeless man rested
on a bench, around him a few compatriots
also sat, the most well-lit picnic
in the world, and when the street cleaners
began to wash Father Duffy's statue
it was like he grew water wings,
grew massive in the quiet, his proper
size. I looked for the Burger King,
OPEN 24 HOURS EVERY DAY,
and it was closed for renovations.

Today I stepped outside, just after
dinner, crossed the street against the light
over and over and over again.

Today, all the world is 3 am,
every hour of every day.

Settler Listens for the Shape of Absent Rain

I spin on my heels, looking for green fields, looking for spring,
looking for lush lakes and lucidity. Here beauty is beyond grasping,
not vivid green but olive sheen, faces turned waxy, mouths agape,
tongues scorched, throats parched, waiting.

Need pulls at my shedding eyelashes and tenuous neck, need curbs my
voice deep into throat, wrenches laughter into the shape of desire—
hollow and sly.

I have lost the sonsie music inside me, lost to silence the shape of
absent rain, to rivulets left behind in the dust. I was brought here, not
belonging but with longing, I must let the sun in, skin to jerky, nose
to the grind of broken-down diamonds.

To eke, to scratch, to hear the slow pull of wheel across rock, to
scrabble, to place hot hands on concrete, tongue held out to collect
sparse early dew, to listen for the screech of copper taps run dry,
laughter as hope, waiting as prayer.

I lower my eyes, grip tight to what is in front, curl into the shadow
of the single branch risen in the dust, creep under the shade of rocks,
bide my life away. Here, I make virtue of hardness, stay constant only
to the land, dirt-laden air too bare for dreams. I've made a prison so I
can live.

Heavy Into Silence

I am jollity when you call.
Tripping lightly between our words
I fashion sandwiches from syllables,
limbo under emphasis.
We toss accent marks lightly
back and forth, over the line.

All the while my fingers
clench tight, tips drain white
as I weave ragged gossamer,
praying this web will hold steady
as your truth falls heavy
into silence.

I have no freedom to offer.
My cage though gilded,
and one most comfortably
fashioned for my shape, still
holds me in, renders me
unable to free you.

I am powerless to provide
relief, my spine buckles
under a weight you have borne
all your life in outrageous grace.

No whisk nor wing
with which to fashion our
escape. Just wrists to wring

in companionable darkness
where you fashion
your kindness lace.

Your honest pain, also his
pain and hers, the pain
of nations, of children
weeping, of the Earth
weeping, of your tears
falling heavy into silence.

I run out of courage,
I run into an anecdote.
I run out of fortitude,
I run into a punchline.
I run out of endurance,
we pun, we pun, we pun.

I don't know how to hold us
but lightly, our jokes leavened
with levity, with space for
tears and rage and everything
in between, as I fall with you.

Don't Ask

my popo says   don't ask   popo says
a man she thought was   Jesus told her the meaning of life
at the bus stop   shelter wall busted
nubby bits of glass   all around
he punch-marked her ticket and said
                           god surely loves you too

what did he mean popo?   she said, don't you know by now baby
she said, your sort—my sort   our sort
we don't ask   they don't tell
you just know   and he told me
                           god surely loves me too

what he meant was   what she thought he meant was
all the no good men   the no good luck
the nobody ever done   right by her   life
but he knew   the poor baby
eyes all open   fresh bloom
she was married at sixteen it was the war
they sent the girls   little girls   little women
to homes in town   away   away
kept away   from the jungle fighters
the ones left behind   breast legs   wide   open
don't ask   and they won't tell
she was sent   away
she said, last lucky thing to ever happen to her

from between her legs   spilling fresh blooms
what to do   with all the blooms
do she do with all these   red red blooms
don't ask   they won't tell
stanch the children   stanch all the children
a girl   a girl   a girl   a boy   a girl
a pig   a horse   a donkey   a prince   an ox

my mama says   don't ask   mama says
a man she thought was   Jesus told her the meaning of life
at the bus stop   shelter walls busted
twisted metal   all around
he scanned the barcode on her ticket   and said
god surely loves you too

what did he mean mama?   she said, don't you know by now baby
she said, your sort—my sort   our sort
we don't ask   they don't tell
we just get on with it   and he told me
god surely loves me too .

us chew the table scraps   cause our jaws tougher kind
us don't go past   high school kind
us send money to send   our brothers to college kind
did you know god   was an architect?
mama wanted to be   an architect too
make forest—skyscrapers   but not women's bodies'
breast legs wide open   designed for what?
we don't ask   they don't tell
our sort   gets on with it and
god surely loves us too

i became the kind of   architect mama said to be
i say—i don't ask—i say   when is it my turn?
they say   oooooooh
so you're god's gift   to the industry   now
but all i was asking for   was what
the boy   the boy   the boy   the   boy   already had

don't ask mama says   don't ask popo says
they're poaching eggs   in the lunch-room
turning tea   into roses
they say don't   get too big for your britches now
they say you   get called up when they want you now
they say don't   you know by now baby
we don't ask   they don't tell
now go back   to the end of the line

i ask when   is it our turn?
i ask how   do we get a turn?
i ask why   girl girl girl boy oxen?
i ask how   to stop this red bloom spreading?
i ask how   do i know when god loves me too?
i ask how   do i know god surely loves us too?

in

The Last Time My Therapist Smashed Everything I Know About Myself Into Ruins

I tell Phil, she's done it again.

Left me

in ruins, my eyes

peeking over broken piles

of bricks, a crow circling overhead

looking for the birdbath I put in the last

time I had to rebuild myself from the ground up

It was a wrecking ball this time, but at least she *left*

foundations. Time before that, even the footings had been ripped up, every rooted memory I'd used to stand up my home was found out, the neon nightmare of every room in the house locked from the outside, the percussion of palm on cheek, the perfect pitch of broken glass whistling inches from teeth. Nothing to be done but build again, this time a palace, this time a home, a different set of histories muddled, this time knives hidden. Try Lego, Phil says, try a spaceship, try an artist' studio, try a hideout for a motorcycle gang. But I root around in the rubble, and

there's something
under   here
that's   still
burning.

Rose Tico

For Kelly Marie Tran, the first Asian American woman and first woman of colour to portray a leading character in a Star Wars film.

FADE IN:
1 SPACE:

> SMALL GIRL (V.O.)
> A small girl, first time at the movies.
> Against a background of starbursts,
> text scrolling into the infinite, my
> first poetry.

2 INT. A MOVIE THEATRE CIRCA 1983 - AFTERNOON:

> SMALL GIRL
> And I fall headlong into a hormonal
> hurricane. I mean, am I a Luke kinda
> girl? Or a Solo kinda girl? Or maybe -
> a Leia kinda girl?

3 INT. A MOVIE THEATRE CIRCA 2012 - NIGHT:

> BIG GIRL (V.O.)
> A big girl, again at the movies, I'm
> there for the later early sequels, or
> is it the earlier late prequels?

                    BIG GIRL

Rebel renegade Rose Tico cannonballs the
scene in her mustard jumpsuit, rounded
cheeks hardened in determination. I'd seen
a dozen trailers, I should know what to
expect and yet, tears astound my cheeks.

                 SMALL GIRL (V.O.)

I mean, who cries at a space opera, right?

                    BIG GIRL

In this wondrous galaxy, shadow anthem of
my youth, heart bursts into starlight the
first time I see:
          (vehemently)
A girl! Who looks! Like me!
          (whispering)
I exist! I am real! Can you see?

4 INT. BY THE LIGHT OF A COMPUTER MONITOR - NIGHT:

                    BIG GIRL

It doesn't take long for the bitter, bite-
sized reddit headlines to reach me, 'Fat
Asian Bitch Ruins Movie'. YouTube provides
further illumination.
          (reads from monitor)
'THAT Fat Asian Bitch Ruined MY Movie.'

(looks into camera)

The collected acid emissions of a generation of angry young white men, that have, up till now, owned the world.

SMALL GIRL (V.O.)

In this wondrous galaxy, I once thought I belonged because - anyone can be a space cowboy! Right?

BIG GIRL

Now I wonder how I ever missed that no one here looks - like me.

5 EXT. CANTO BIGHT:

BIG GIRL

Now, Rose Tico and me, standing on the parapet of Canto Bight watching you, a big boy, at the movies. Rebel renegade Rose Tico cannonballs the scene, rips through the monochrome of your galaxy.

ROSE TICO

Maybe the one place you are not fodder for bullies. Where the magic you believe in with all your heart is consistent with strength, with heroism. Where you can live up to your father's roaring admonishment to 'Be a man!'

                    BIG GIRL
     Here men cry, and fail, get beaten,
     pick up their light sabres and win!
     Here, you belong, because anyone can
     be a space cowboy, right?

6 EXT. STARSHIP COCKPIT:

                    BIG GIRL
     Rose Tico and me in the cockpit of a
     starship watching you, a small boy,
     first time at the movies. Against a
     background of starbursts, Luke kisses
     Leia, Solo swaggers, you fall headlong
     into hurricane.
               (tenderly)
     A Boy! Who looks! Like you!
               (looks into camera)
     You exist. You are real. I see.

FADE OUT.

It's 1:44am

and I'm eating cold chicken in front of the fridge,
stabbing my fork into white breast,
cold Pyrex slippery with condensation,
the shhhhck of flesh pulling away from bone.

Shiny prongs thrust into soft breast,
the insistent scraping of tines on glass,
slick flesh pulling away from bone,
grease melting on ravenous tongue.

Scratches etched deep into glass,
from the back of the fridge, a mechanical hum,
meat sweetly coaxed between teeth and tongue,
a gnawing for only the hours after midnight.

In the dark quiet, the fridge clicks and hums,
throat thrown back in wheezing rapture,
a precise hunger fills the hours after midnight.
I used to eat granola for dinner.

Throat drawn tight in guilty rapture,
shoulders rounded, a carcass stripped bare,
I used to eat granola in front of the telly,
mother called it a dirty habit.

Neck tucked in, a carcass unveiled,
if I wanted the sun, I would have made it,
mother called it a dirty habit,
she used to raid the fridge past midnight.

If I wanted the sun, I would have swallowed it,
a cold dish, greasy with condensation,
she'd harvest dinner past midnight,
eating cold chicken in front of the fridge.

Hide and Go Seek

When I'm at the self-checkout
machine at Woolies
spinning my cans around and around
in a game of barcode
hide go seek.
I often get the sly impulse
to slip the last packet of sausages
the cheap ones
the ones that shrivel in the pan
usually $3.80
straight into my bag
right past the red seeing eye dog
barcode facing forward
all filler, no chiller
weight imperceptible
step heft step out the
—sliding door.

I mean I'd never
no never have, never will
but that thought
—flashes...
Oh, you don't get
that impulse?
It sounds slightly
criminal?
Me either
something I've heard
slippery slope

and all that.
'nother round?

When I'm driving forty-nine
in a fifty zone
and a pigeon waddles across
the pedestrian lane
I often get the impulse
to accelerate
to clip a wing
see it spin
like a grey and white top
not hurt but dizzy
carrying my prayers on its
winging dervish.
Why did the pigeon
cross the road?
To go home.

I mean I'd never
no never have, never will
snaps its fingers
—moves me…
Oh you don't ever—
would never occur—
it's sadistic?
Me either
something on the news
these tendencies
sometimes hereditary
proof of criminality
matter of time.

You're what I want to be
when I grow up
restraint, and a free-wheeling
interest in bark.
Not that other
sneak thief
bird slayer
my own greedy
envious and spiteful tics
grown too large
from playing hide go seek
to hide.

Go.
Seek.

Golden Boy

You glowed in the light
of my solar yearning.
Basked, took a tan,
dug your toes into my
golden sand crush.

I bought you a cone
from the ice cream van,
whispered that I
really really liked you.
Your smile promised
ditto.

Was it foolish then?
I was surprised when
my best friend Rachel reported
her first kiss
on the same beach
behind the ice cream van
with you.

You told me you didn't
think it mattered.

Golden boy,
I'd forgotten the power
of being in love
on the lighter side of eighteen.

Is it foolish now?
I haven't forgotten
the sunburn sting.
I have never since
gotten so close to the sun.

Blue Light

This is a rare dawn poem.
I am never the one to pad
around the house drawing up
the blinds, that is his

domain. Yesterday he slammed
fists into the steering wheel,
shouted why do you need
me to say what you already

know. Magpies chanting
through the dawn light in my
window wonders why I am up,
not still under the covers

praying for a little more
get-up-and-go-go-go. They
don't see here in the blue, I am
allowed the light in my eyes.

Small Revolutions

Riding home in the cold-dark, the regular
                       revolution of feet to pedal on ground.
A careless alignment of tyre with the groove
              of tram tracks brings my bicycle to ground.

A skid of forward motion, the evolution into
                 tumbling, a fall slowed to imperceptibility
by a body bracing for the battering brunt
              of skin and bone against shattered ground.

The streets were silent before, near curfewed,
               the guilty surge towards home interrupted
by this thicker silence, the density of cold
              molasses, the dark of asphalt-paved ground.

The screech of tyres-sudden-braked, confusion
              of wrist-right-angle-to-fingers, head
bobbing heedlessly for apples suddenly
              withdrawn like treats from grounded

children. The tongue is piqued first by sugar,
              then by salt, then insulted by a bitterness
elusive as the excitable pollution of melted
              bitumen at the vacant playground.

The relief in the finality of pain as I settle
              into the sidewalk, it seeks and finds kindness

in the man who stops his car, furnishes
>   me with water, bandages and common ground.

And as stopped heart beats again, for the first
>   time in two hundred days I remember
that I am alive, that I am Beloved, abraded
>   palms outstretched between sky and ground.

hold

His-and-Hers Sinks

It's a double sink, 'his-and-hers' sink. The basins are cold and smooth. I lay each baby in a basin, checking their swaddles are tight. I lay them just like that, 'his-and-hers', the boy on the left near the edge with the slot for his shaver, the girl on the right with the ledge for all her bottles of cosmetics and cream. I cradle them into their sinks and wrap myself with the torn shower curtain, its edges pink and black with mould. I lay down in the bathtub to sleep.

The lights are still on when I wake up. Even though the morning sun is streaming in through the small, cracked window in the corner. As I get up, I remember not to hit my head on the bath tap. It's a nice bathroom, much nicer than I'm used to. The faucets are brass and shiny. The mirror isn't misted with spittle and toothpaste. Even the bath mat is still plush.

Except for this shower curtain, pink and slimy. One of the babies whimper and I remember they are here.

I take a drink from the faucet.

I remember my arm wrapped in my coat last night, striking. The jagged break in the bathroom window. The babies were crying where I lay them. I picked them up, each a warm, damp weight in my arms, they shushed.

But I don't remember where 'here' is.

They are both whimpering now. Even though I found this sink for them, perfect for two, 'his-and-hers' sink for him and her, just their size. Their mouths round and gaping, like sink drains, both faces mottled purple and pink, the colour of the tiles.

Everything in this bathroom matches, even the towels over the his-and-hers sink.

I think I haven't shaved my legs in months, I am disgusting. I find the razor under the sink. It is in a neat, blue mug, the handle broken. I sit at the edge of the tub. I tell the babies to shush.

There is a knocking at the door, I can't answer it, I'm shaving my legs.

The knocking gets louder. I can hear it over the babies' wailing. I don't remember where 'here' is. But I am not done. I am careful to shave every inch.

I am done shaving, but they are still crying. I can't remember where 'here' is. I wash the razor carefully in the bathtub.

The babies haven't settled. I wonder if their swaddles are too tight. I unwrap them.

The knocking strikes like drumbeats. I turn on the faucets, the sound of water is soothing. I press the rubber plugs, round and smooth like baby bellies, into the sink drains. I watch the water rise.

The babies are still crying.

I can't remember where this is.

Minutae

The oranges stink sweet and citrus,
you aren't here to peel them.
Dirty dishes decay in the sink,
I've only heart to wash glasses.

No one here to taste for salt,
every dish I make is peppered
and listless, my heart swollen
to fill my stomach.

I found the curry
you left in the freezer for me.
Did you find
the sweater I packed?

Third Drawer Down

Have I lived enough
to have anything worth saying?
Read enough books, seen
enough sunsets in far flung places,
if the wind has blown enough
dirt into my nostrils?

Does wisdom grow each time
I am cut or bled? Does worth swell
with frequency? With intensity?
Perhaps the proper measure
is identity—of the person
who did the cutting.

Do I have enough kitchen implements
used once and now catching on the lip
of the third drawer down?
Begged enough times for my life
or for the end of life, collected enough
accolades or broken seashells?

Do I have enough old photographs
hidden in dusty drawer backs?
    Taken enough abuse aimed
and delivered through car windows?
    Have I drunk enough soup
    beer or gin? Thrown up on

    unfamiliar doorways, s t a g g e r e d
      into smelly cabs with vaguely
        menacing strangers.

Does it count if I've wandered the lovely streets with

balloons tied to the edge of my gown?

You Do Not Even
Know My Name

Sure, you brought me
to this place, signed
the papers, said the mole
under my eye was the mark
of a tearful life.

But I made myself from what
bittersweet I could find, shrivelled
olives at the back of the pantry,
. a mason jar of glazed
cherries in the cabinet of old

Tupperware, and the cans of Spam
everyone buys for camping trips
and pandemics except—when
was the last time anyone went
camping? I cut out my eyes,

made salty sandwiches in lieu
of tears, the mole is still
there, Have you looked
lately? It is the shape
of molted wings.

The Frog Apocalypse

after Melinda Smith's 'The Sausage Dog Apocalypse'

It will happen not far from here.

All the tiny green frogs in my carefully cultivated garden will rise up
and with one mighty, final croak - go silent forever,
and instead form a picket line
by the chrysanthemums
demanding cat food

and the anthill under the drain cover will finally reach the light,
years of secret building, the season of drought
is their time to rise

and angry men with toast crumbs in their beards will throw the doors
open, march through our study in their steel capped boots,
flipping the bird as they pass
our family photographs

and the world's consortium of geckoes will stop amusing babies
with their chirrups, and with perfectly formed vowels
will chant anti-capitalist slogans
in unison

and children stricken by the most recent pandemic, will storm
the hospital wards in search of a tapestry
made of beer bottle tops

and bee-keepers everywhere will set fire to their hives, honey
will adhere like tar to the inside of
every eyelid

and we will sleep
in burnt caramel dreams

and despite being unable to see through sticky eyelids, or hear
through ears choked in pollen, I will appreciate
my proper weightlessness,
stop hogging space on the couch, send a can
of tomatoes crashing through
the television screen

and joining the frogs in solidarity, I will recover
the perfect pen from behind the chrysanthemums,

and I will write

a poem proper in its solitude, impossible to recite
quietly enough to express
its insignificance

The Promise

after 'Rhythm 0' by Marina Abramovic

you / we begin
with ~~nothing~~ one
you are
    a rose is a blade is a rose
each timid kiss
    honeyed lips
anticipated sweetness
    hands on body
a slow dance

your / my body   pushed
                    pulled
your / my body   caressed
                    cut
your / my body   licked
                    lingered
they hate us for how~~l~~
we take their punishment
(mirror mirror)

a knife at the throat
    blood   kiss   stolen
like a lover
a knife between your legs
    body   leaden   dragged
like a corpse
seventy two objects
    each ~~one~~ threatens

rape death
the hand that wields
is weak~~ened~~
your / my body   is
          monstrous
your / my body
          the shot that lets
          the foul in
I / we promise   to be
          monstrous

Double Knot

I got the news in an aerogramme, thin
and slippery as onion skin between my fingers,

the first time my friend killed herself.
She left me holding a small tattered

bundle of misunderstanding. I missed
what she was telling me about her

new friends, why she got me to pinky swear
to name my first child after her. In this

> *I failed you. There is no child and I wonder*
> *who will remember your name when I am gone.*

She was eight thousand miles away, the caller's
voice warm and tentative in my ear.

the second time my friend killed herself.
They didn't know if the overdose

was intentional, or if she forgot an earlier dose,
or was just indulging the need to sleep.

We scattered her ashes, and each chose
a piece from her jewellery box. I picked

> *the silver turtle I'd gifted you that time*
> *you left us to run away from yourself.*

A year later I found out she'd hung herself,
no accident, that elaborate double knot.

Things I've Lost

Innocence, that old cliche.
Eight bobby pins in the last
year, before I cut my hair.
Twelve years of journal entries,
deleted off a distant server
when an Internet site went bust.

They say Rachel Tuck lost her verve,
when her body began
to be riddled with tumours.
I wonder what verve feels like,
if I have it and can I ever
know before it's gone.

I've lost three months
wages and a bankrupt boss.
Eleven colour pencils from a set
of a dozen, the remaining colour
being green, as grass
featured rarely in my

colouring-ins, filled as they are with orange
people, yellow
sand, blue
skies, red
petals, and well worn white
clouds etched into bleached paper.

I've lost eighteen hundred random
dreams, dropped in the space
behind the bed, that gap between
waking and replacing the cap
on the toothpaste.
All the photographs

from a Japanese vacation,
the vividness from recollections
of elegant pagodas
and rosy salmon sashimi.

Also misplaced, a sense
of wonder at being alive.
And decorum.
Loss leaving in its place
a lusty love
for the glorious,
utilitarian versatility
of the word

fuck.

Scar Tissue

You lead me through strange geographies.
You say, up here the tide
cannot drown our sandwiches.
You say, up here you can see
where salt scarred the land.
I tell you, my steps follow
your footfalls.
I don't say, I can only drink
where the rocks have cut my veins.
I don't say, here:
I am a snail without my shell.

You lead me to new territories.
You say, all our wandering lives
we have trained for thinner air.
You say, sun fire will not scar
the brave.
I tell you, my steps follow
your footfalls.
I don't say, I am invisible
without the waves to speak my shape.
I don't say, ash has filled my mouth
and I cannot breathe.

Where Do I Carry Life

Where does it lurk, a lifetime seeking yields no fixed address, so it must hide in plain sight, must keep moving; the shoulder blades, the back of neck, in a curve of spine, briefly resting on the top lip of a smile before it springs onto the left big toe, balance and fire. Surely we could be friends, but no it likes that I bear it, dragging its dead weight as heavy as my full self across days, congealed and patterned. Even as I sleep, seeking relief in darkness it dances in my veins pumping, always pumping making muzak through my dream sound system never alone for an instant. Until the instant I am alone. How quiet that will be.

This Poem Contains Ramen

This poem contains ramen.

    It contains ramen because I am living in this poem / and these days the only thing I crave is ramen / So much so, when my economist / asks me what I want for dinner / there is only ever one answer / I don't even know why he asks anymore / I guess it's one of our rituals / And I might change my mind / after all, there were those three years / when all I wanted to eat was laksa.
So now this poem contains that as well,
but only in a nostalgic, past particular way.

This poem also contains my economist,

    at least the parts of him that asks me / what I want for dinner, and the part of him / that is unquenchably hopeful / that sees the world as a rational problem / of limited resources and unlimited wants / and if we could only find the right model / we could solve the problem with Pi / I also think pie solves most problems / especially on those frigid nights / when the cold makes my toe itch / My itchy toe is also in this poem.
So is pi(e).

This poem contains ramen,

    with the kind of ramen soup that / clings to the rounded back of spoons / wraps noodles, wraps my lips / in hot, delicious fat, dances on my tongue / with umami. This poem now contains a taste / that didn't even exist before it was / discovered? created? by the inventor of MSG / What did we taste before we had a word for it? / Could we taste it at all? / Could I invent another taste right now? / Inside this poem? I bet I can / Seus. (The 's' is silent.)
I declare it to be (in this poem).

It's the taste of being at the park / and seeing a kite fly so high
and so far / that all of the the sky and the grass / and the dogs running
/ and the joy of all things far and wide / and beyond your reckoning /
pours into your soul through your mouth / That's seus (the 's' is silent)
/ Now here come the hipsters and clever chefs / searching for the taste
of seus (the 's' is silent) / They are having conferences in this poem /
authoring research papers, fanning controversy.
Is seus real? Is it mass hypnosis?

You could say its cheating
putting my own-self into a poem.
       It only proves how much of a noodle I am.
Yet Thomas put his whole dying father
into a poem, into a villanelle no less,
       that dying father more alive than most people I know
       living outside of poems.
I am no Thomas, so I must cut my cloth
to fit myself. And besides, I couldn't bear it,
       if I accidentally suffocated someone else
       in my poem.
But it's not so bad, inside this poem.
After all, it contains   ramen.

Oxbow Lake

                    I felt your eyebrows arch
                when I said everything
                I am comes from her.

                    Everything? you said,
                And where is there
                room for you?   But

                    you weren't there
                        when she drew the S
                        of a river bend, explained

                        how the river grows
                        sluggish with too much
                            water, forms swollen bellies.

                        How when the mouth
                        has swallowed enough silt,
                        the river straightens in its rush

                            to the sea, and here
                        with a pencil stroke,
                        she cuts a body

                            shaped like
                            a kidney
                            from its
                            source.

Proof

for AL and NK

Imagine the scene: you are a small child watching your mother /
grandmother / cousin / great uncle, slam their head against a brick
wall, throw fast money at slow horses, find reason with unreasonable
men, draw frenetic flame through lungpipes for the only kind of
high they can feel, and on and on and on — each one of you in turn,
passing a treasured inheritance down with the family resemblance.

With each turn, the silent pleading with the gods, any of the gods,
how do you stop this turn, the next, and the next, your turn, her turn,
his turn, do your children get a turn, are you all to be swept along,
watching the interminable, banal horror spool into a lifetime or two
or three, every day with its small doses? There is no possible turning.
You are a small child watching your first true love's dissolution.

Love is another word for a hostage negotiation. What do you care
about so much, you would be willing to sacrifice yourself for its
survival? Will you rend your small heart into pieces to believe you
are loved? Let your soul spill down a swirling sinkhole to hide your
wounds from yourself?

But here you are, body, at once child, and adult, looking upon the
scene through hazy memory. Realise that you are here — in the
present, even as you have abandoned both split heart and spilt soul in
the past particular. How, body, did you get to this space-time that is
the only place you can hold breath?

Here you are, on your own feet, all the turns of time you have been seeking unceasingly for the true shape of your small self, for the sound of hope playing in trauma's careless breath, for the fresh faint scent of healing laced through generational disaster, for love on the topside of every backhand. How, body, did you get to this filigree reality, constructed from cracked and unreliable debris?

It is now you remember the bridges that have spanned every treacherous crossing: the friend who believed you before you believed yourself, the teacher who juddered your jaw with this truth — that no love can reach you if you don't first love yourself, the therapist who challenged your cruelty relentlessly, the fairy godmother bestowing upon you only the wisdom your body could bear, the lover who forgave you for not being able to forgive.

You walked yourself out of that scene, body, and now you remember hands waiting to receive you, ears willing you to hear yourself, eyes softened into mirrors, your small past prayers answered at every turn, always when you least expected it.

You are alive. Thrillingly, tenderly so. And what is that if not proof of the love you've been seeking?

Acknowledgements

Poems in this collection have previously appeared in the following journals and publications: 'Scar Tissue' in *Rabbit, no 33, Asia, 2021* and *Best of Australian Poems 2022 (Australian Poetry, 2022)*, 'Clot & Marrow' and 'Double Knot' in *Poetry of Encounter (Liquid Amber Press, 2023)*, 'Elephant' and 'Gasping' in *Kalliope X, Issue 3, Spring 2022*, 'The Last Time my Therapist Smashed Everything I Know into Ruins' in *Admissions: Voices within Mental Health (Upswell Publishing, Oct 2022)*, 'My Voice through Your Ears' in *Borderless: A Transnational Anthology of Feminist Poetry (Recent Work Press, July 2021)*, 'Pregnancy and the Bikini Wax' in *What We Carry: Poetry on Childbearing (Recent Work Press, May 2021)*, 'Women's Histories' in *No News: 90 Poets Reflect on a Unique BBC Newscast (Recent Work Press, April 2020)*, 'Back to You' in *Verity La*, 'Serviettes' in *Australian Poetry Anthology Vol 7 2019*, 'Double Sinks' in *Australian Poetry Journal vol 8.2 2018*, 'spoken, 'Don't Ask' in *Cold Mountain Review Fall 2018* and *Australian Poetry Anthology 2020*.

'Clot & Marrow' and 'Double Knot' were shortlisted in Liquid Amber Press 2022 Poetry Prize by Liquid Amber Press, 2023.

'The Frog Apocalypse' was highly commended in 2019 Open Section, Woorilla Poetry Prize.

Thank you to the tireless and unlauded editors, publishers, anthologists and curators—who nourish the ecosystem for poets to be heard and read.

Poetry is inseparable from community for me and I owe a deep debt of gratitude to so many, only a few mentioned below…

Teachers, mentors and guiding lights Andy Jackson and Sam Ferrante, who through many (many!) drafts—through their own poetry, the way they conduct their lives and engage with community—have modelled for me how to do the necessary work with joy, courage and commitment.

This book and these poems are much improved for the generosity and genius of Arielle Cottingham, Claire Gaskin, Judith Rodriguez (deeply missed), Henry Briffa, Jacqui Malins (for advice on book structure), Loran Steinberg, Melizarani T. Selva, Phillip Kent-Hughes (for pushing me across the Rubicon), Steve Smart, Will Beale, Abigail Johnson, JD Amick, Logan Taylor and Scoot Swain.

The Naarm spoken word and poetry community: I miss those nights under the hammer, when 3 hour workshops turned into 5 hour poetry jams, staying up too late, voices falling in embrace of a red-eyed couplet, rising in defence of a metaphor, dropping bits of cold pizza and cheap red wine on tired sofas, someone always sprawled on the carpet, someone huddled close to the heater, never enough crackers for the dip. The last tram rumbling past, we always meant to catch it but almost never did. You taught me the shape of a line, the resonance of a fractured stanza, the potential in the perfect image, the ethics of ideas, how to be utterly ruthless and endlessly kind. We were talking about art, but really, we were talking about community and passion and meaning and life and love. You know who you are. You are in my heart.

Incomparable editor, publisher and friend Shane Strange, for your belief in me, for your knack of saying the right word at the right time, and for successfully wrestling this out of my death grip.

Anna and Ambika, for loving me whilst making sure I keep it real.

Bill and Bryon, for walking me across the darkness.

Arthur, who believed in me long before I believed in myself.

To the Reader and Listener of Poetry, you Rock!

About the Author

Es Foong (Waffle Irongirl) is a poet, writer and spoken word performer living in Naarm. Their poems have appeared in *Australian Poetry Journal*, *Rabbit Poetry, Kalliope X* and the *Best of Australian Poems 2022* anthology. They have performed on poetry stages including Passionate Tongues, La Mama Poetica and Queensland Poetry Festival 2022. On-stage, they are the poetic analogue of heavy-metal karaoke. Off-stage, they eat identity labels for breakfast. They live online at waffleirongirl.com.

www.ingramcontent.com/pod-product-compliance
Ingram Content Group Australia Pty Ltd
76 Discovery Rd, Dandenong South VIC 3175, AU
AUHW020721050325
407891AU00005B/25